Urban Daylight

Poetry

Letters From My Soul

Brenda Wilborn

outskirts
press

Table of Contents

1. I Love Your Beautiful Mind

You stimulate the neurons in my brain
Exciting my frontal lobes
Giving my cerebral cortex butterflies
Awakening my third eye
Enabling my pineal gland
I love the way you intrigue me
And all the beautiful things
You say to entice me
Eloquently caressing
My ears with
Soft syllables and
Seductive metaphors
You enlighten me
You help me create lyrically
Massaging my ego with
Kind words and smooth gestures
Undressing me with explicit
After-dark midnight conversations
Making my head spin
Got me flowing poetically
I am ready to carry your seeds
And give birth to
A whole new generation
Of kings and queens
Leaving the old and
Creating everything new
I want to build kingdoms
And pyramids with you
I can see us on golden thrones
Living in magnificent castles
Cultivated from the finest stones
And now I find myself

Sitting like a flower in
Full bloom advertising
My sweet nectar patiently
Waiting for you to
Gently kiss each petal
Once more
I'm auditioning for you
Mi amor

I Love Your Beautiful Mind

2. Honey Dip Man

It's almost sunrise
Our smiles greet each other
I turn over and move my hair away
From your eyes you grab
Me around my waist
And pull me in closer to you
Then you softly
Whisper in my ear and gently
Kiss me on the nape
Of my neck and taste my
Lips just before the sun
Peeks above the golden
Horizon
We lie on a bed
Of roses surrounded by
A canopy of fresh air and
Robust fumes of early morning dew
The window is still open
And we succumb to the
Warm breeze as it brushes
Our damp skin from the night before
You offer me serenity and
Pleasure like no other man has ever done
Exceeding all of my expectations stroking my
Upper Peninsula perfectly
Giving me a legitimate excuse
To overindulge in you
Hypnotizing me with
Sexy mind-blowing interludes
Brilliantly laced with romance
And steamy hot passion
When we make love you

Leave behind a beautiful
Collage of colorful love
Murals that stain my womb
We meticulously explore each other's
Flesh on higher grounds
We become equally yoked
Pretending to be a sponge I
Soak up all your sweet juice
No longer standing still
We manipulate time
Fast-forwarding into reality
Reinventing our future moving stagnant
Mountains and surrendering all
To love boldly
Making the earth shake
Calming my ferocious
Appetite taming my
Aggressive hunger pangs
Settling an old score
I'm not finished with you
Honey Dipped Man
I still want more

3. Soul Mate

I don't need to wear
A mask with you I
Can be free, natural and
Naked in front of you
You make it so easy for
Me to live in my truth
Allowing my authenticity to
Shine through brilliantly
I can wear my emotions
Out in the open when
I am with you I
Carefully pull back the
Layers of my soul without
Any judgment, ridicule or
Persecution from you
Helping me to
Trust my heart
I become my best self
You always seem to say
Whatever I am thinking
Knowing my thoughts
Before I speak them
You stay inside my head
Making me run wild in
The garden of my mind
Constantly planting your
Beautiful seeds there
Enabling me to water and
Intellectually cultivate them
Watching as they blossom
Into lovely deep-rooted
Fruits of opportunity
Refreshing my perspective

Widening my lens
Letting me see the world
In a different light
We connect harmoniously
On every level
From the very beginning
You were my foundation
You are the platform
That keeps me elevated
Your unconventional knowledge
Gracefully renders
Lessons in patience and understanding
You push me towards
My goals and you want
The best for me
You believe in me
And my dreams
Accepting my metamorphosis
Acknowledging my genius
Gifts and strengths being
Confident and mature
Enough to let my
Light shine without
Trying to dim it
With you by my side
I become greatness
With ease
You become the center
Of my universe
I become your beautiful
Lotus flower
You are my sunset
My evening star
The love of my life
You are my soul mate

4. Hypnotic

You woo me with
Your ingenious mind-blowing devices
Attracting my attention
With your unpredictable
Character
I love all of your
Flamboyant eccentricities
Dazzling me with your exotic image and
Scandalous behavior
Courting me with showmanship
Seducing & enthralling me
With your larger-than-life
Commodities
You hypnotize me
With flavorful charm and
Delight me with
Your unorthodox flair
You give sunlight to all of my
Beautiful imaginations
You constantly excite and
Heighten all of my interests
You look at me with the
Crescent moon in your eyes
Your mysterious and hard-
To-grasp intentions have me
In a whirlwind trying to
Interpret you
Carefully controlling your words
You leave behind an air of
Intrigue
Clairvoyance is the name
Of your sweet seduction

Fascinating me with all
Kinds of optical illusions
You plan methodically
And pace your momentum
Strategically and deliberately
Then you brilliantly
Execute your plan
Luring me in with ease
Eliciting love from me
Conquering and overpowering
My flesh like a prowling
Hungry untamed savage beast
Forcing sweet submission
Sealing the ties that bind
Winning the challenge
Finally, the chase is over
You make me love you without regulation
You accomplish masterfully
I am yours forever and
You will always belong to me

5. Return

What once was
Has begun again
Memories take a toll
Giving my heart
Colossal hope
Unyielding in its
Gratifying propensity
I knew you would
Return to me
Or could this be
You're playing a deceptive
Game of you hide
And I go seek
Oh...how I wish...
To mount thee...
Exclusively...
Riding gliding and
Sliding off into the sunset
Getting reacquainted
On the beautiful wings
Of ecstasy's peak
We lose ourselves
In the moment and
Rekindle our
Precious bond
Making it secure
I've been longing to give
You what you came for
Something so rare
Magical delicate delicious
Beautiful mysterious and pure
You

Me
We
Us
Together
Forever
In Sync
Harmoniously

6. Afrocentric Kind of Love

You got that
Good good strong
Gangsta hood
Turn a woman
Out kind of love
That Oooh... Weeeee...
He did his thang
Kind of love
That making me
Feel like I wanna
Let you pull my hair
Kind of love
That I wanna
Be with you
For LIFE
Until I die
Kind of love
That making me
Dream about you
Kind of love
That feel so good
Don't ever stop
Kind of love
That making me
Wanna smoke
Some green haze
With yo ass and
Listen to Future's
Beast Mode mixtape
CD while I
Let you freak
Me all night long

Kind of love
That I never felt
Like this before
Kind of love
That got me feeling
All kinds of sexy
And seductive
Kind of love
That mmmm baby
Hold on tight cause
Here we go
Kind of love
That making thighs
Blush and quiver
Kind of love
That making tears
Stream from my
Eyes kind of love
That tender and
Very gentle let
Me please you
Anyway you desire
Kind of love
That I wanna
Build with you forever
Kind of love
That massage
Your hands... shoulders...
Back... feet... and have
Your bath water ready
Every night
Kind of love
That cook you
A full course
Homemade meal

From scratch three
Times a day
With your favorite
Dessert on the side
Kind of love
That have your
Favorite Mexican
Beer in my hand
Ice cold with
A slice of lime
Ready for you as
Soon as you come
Home from work
Kind of love
That you bet not
Get up to answer
That phone and I
Don't care if it
Is your mama calling
Kind of love
That whimsical
Floating throughout
The galaxies
Sitting on the moon
Kind of love
That raw unique
And unprecedented
Kind of love
Its days like this
That I will
Forever live for
Cause you got
That Afrocentric
Kind of love

7. All Is Forgiven

Here I go again
Once more
Thinking of you
Remembering how you
Use to gently touch me on
The small of my back
I was so young and innocent
It's almost three decades later and
I can still recall how beautiful and pure you would always make
me feel
Just as if it were yesterday
Got me momentarily
Hot and bothered
Charming me with sweet memories
Catching me off guard
Without warning I
Find myself slipping
Into a deep never-ending
Emotional black abyss
Skyrocketing traveling swiftly
At the speed of sound
Going back in time
Cascading through a steaming
Hot lover's vortex
Putting things in order
Correcting a past drenched
In sorrow and misery
Our time together was
Short-changed many
Words were left unsaid
Taking the higher road
I now speak to you from

My apologetic forgiving heart
Face-to-face
Poetically, linguistically and truthfully, I stand before you naked
With powerful hands that
Hold my head up towards the sky
Baring my intelligent
Lovely soul hoping
That you can still
Hear and feel
The love that resides
Within me
At last, all is forgiven
And all is well
I can finally push
Forward with a smile
On my face
Looking to the heavens for guidance, peace and strength
We failed our test miserably
And yet, I am still forever
Grateful for the empirical lesson
Without looking back
I elevate majestically

8. Beautiful Charm

I stand here counting the
Minutes hours and the days
Until I see you again
The love you give me
Is rare and gentle
You shower me
With it freely
You make me crave you I
Pray to the heavens for
Your time and attention
Different from the others
You appease all of my
Senses in multiple ways
I can feel when you think of me
I see you every night in my dreams
You've got me crying tears of joy
In my sleep, I love the way you
Hold my hand when we take
Our long walks in the sky
You teach me how to
Spread my wings and then
I learn how to fly ever so sweetly
Your generous nature is
Astounding to me
Soothing my anxieties
With gifts and late
Night rooftop dinners
Encased in vintage wine
And fine chocolates
I lose all track of time
When I am near you
I become love struck

And discombobulated
I love your beautiful charm
You stir my memory and
Make it pleasurable to relive
My past with you seducing me
And allowing familiarity to creep in
You make lavender and white
Orchid flower petals fall from between my
Thighs your sweet watermelon-
Flavored kisses overpower me
Sending me into a bioluminescent floating world
Full of tenderness, happiness and mystery
Putting me in remembrance of my
Lovely youthful innocence
You simultaneously learn
All of my peculiarities which
Makes me want you more
My insatiable lust for you
Makes me see
Through rose-colored shades
You stimulate me visually
Intellectually and creatively
You give me foreplay
Months before we
Connect physically making
Me love you with my
Brain and my heart
My inhibitions become
Lowered with you and I
Quickly helplessly
Lose myself in every
Moment with you
Versatility in its purest form
Is what you give to me
I drift along the turquoise rivers

That you create for me
Skillfully I ride the currents
You become my shelter
And my hideaway and I become
Your pretty private cathedral
I betray my moral compass
And give myself to you completely
I wanna be more than
Just your friend I wanna
Be your beginning
And your end

9. Addiction

I am addicted to your sexy unapologetic swag
I get hypnotized when you are with me
I melt like ice when you kiss me
Your dark chocolate body aroma intoxicates me
Your enchanting beauty is amazing
Your brilliance is genius
It mesmerizes me
Your warm chill disposition soothes me
Your mysterious eyes tell me your life story
Then they seduce me
Your sweet touch invites me to become one with you
I anxiously accept the offer
You allure me with your strong personality
When I hear your voice, you make my body quiver (nonstop)
I am smitten by you
You got me flowing like a water fountain
On full atomic blast
Giving me jolts of instantaneous pleasure
Your grind and hustle fascinates me
I see all kinds of colorful fireworks when you caress me
You are like a drug to me
My only drug of choice
I gotta have it (you) my insatiable fix
You be like my love pusher man
I will always oblige you as
Your dedicated hooked love customer
Your love runs through me
It swims through my veins
Especially when you call out my name
I float on air when I am with you
You make me wanna wine and dine in the sky with you
Got me feeling like I can let all my natural kinky curly

Pretty hair down and fly high away with you
I will always let you serve me
You keep me on open for you
I am addicted to only you

10. I Celebrate You

You are breathtaking and phenomenal in every way
Your masculine physique is a work of fine art
A sculptured Michelangelo masterpiece
Your smooth distinctive disposition raises the bar for other men

You make love to my mind, body and soul when you talk to me
You enunciate words perfectly
When I don't hear from you for an hour, it feels like an eternity
You inspire me with your kindness and your cool uncut raw skills

Your sweet seductive soothing energy
Sends me into euphoric bliss
You romance me with your eyes when you look at me
You alter the state of my consciousness
You take me to foreign places in my mind

You have me reciting poetry in my dreams
Making me reach unexpected levels of creativity
You elicit love so easily from me
Forcing me to give you all of my goodies freely

You make beautiful pink rose petals fall from in between my legs
You make all kinds of flowers bloom in my backyard
Your sensual persuasion constantly knocks me off my feet
You always seem to see the best in me

You see past all of my flaws and imperfect ways
You refrain from criticizing or judging me
You inspire and uplift me
You love me unconditionally

I can be my true authentic self when we are together
I don't have to pretend with you
I can feel every millisecond of our history when
You kiss me or touch my hand
You are my Nubian king, comfort and peace

"Today I celebrate you, my lover and friend."

11. "Flight No. 30"

I waited 30 years to step aboard your flight
And now you are here teaching me
How to fly once more
I buckle up to prepare
For the most intoxicating
Splendid ride of my life
I can sense your insatiable hunger
To have me again and
You quickly make it known
I watch and feel you navigate
My terrain so wondrously
Making each moment feel perfect
Giving me tender rolling tongue
Bottom lip sucking
Belly button sensational kisses that momentarily
Take my breath away and
Sweltering interludes of pleasure
Meticulously touching every geographical location
I am in awe of your magnificent aviation
Lovely candlelight dinners in
Beautiful magenta-colored skies
We mingle with shining stars as
We sit on top of purple clouds
I love our expedited rendezvous
We both begin to soar
I can see strawberry-colored winds
Blowing through my hair
I now revisit high altitude places
Where I have already been in my mind
With you
Got me feeling like I can stand
On top of the world

Making me feel invincible
My heart is smiling at you
This flight No. 30 celebration
Will never end

12. Monsoon Rains

I see gentle iridescent monsoon raindrops
Whenever I am near you
Falling nonstop
I get thunderstruck and speechless
When you smell and touch my natural hair
Telling me it's soft and that it smells like
Strawberries and peppermint cotton candy
I love the way you nervously touch my hair
You do it so gently
When I look at you, I can feel your heart
Beating to a natural authentic Congo rhythm
Your whimsical kisses knock
Me off my feet
Got me all unbalanced and dizzy
I am reveled by your very sensual nature
I find myself constantly changing my
Hairstyles attempting to impress you
Wanting to remain forever indigenous
Only for you
Always weaving me up in your
Infinite webs of curiosity
You cradle my every sense on demand
You empower me with every embrace
And you don't even know it
Forcing me to rule and reign by
Boldly stepping into
My artistic creativity
Aligning me with my destiny
I must admit that you help me
Reach my destinations so beautifully
I can feel your love for me with every plunge
You got my body levitating in the air

Soaring through the universe on one of
Your fantasy galactic wave flights
And then we both arrive
Satisfying my raging hunger
You somehow manage to disappear again
I still suffer from chills and night sweats
Making me wake up at 2 am in the morning
Looking all disheveled hoping to see you
Parked in my driveway sitting in your
Cream-colored '98 ole skool Cadillac Coupe DeVille
You give me wonderful sleep-walking sensations but
It's not reality because you're just an illusion
You're not here permanently and you
Never will be so I guess I will continue to see and feel
Monsoon rains that you so passionately
Give to me

13. Lovely Initiation

You serenade me with your hood game
Introducing me to unprecedented realms of mind-blowing ecstasy
Liberating my soul at the slightest touch
You amaze me with your ghetto etiquette
Performing acrobatic tricks in my mouth
With your sweet golden tongue
Infusing me with your love potion
Sultry endeavors are no longer a fantasy
My thoughts become my reality
I quickly submit to your masterful explicit
Lovely time travel
Merging our spirit and flesh together
The excursion begins
You've got me suspended in the air
Floating in beautifully colored winds
Upside down
I reach new horizons
Making my body vibrate on a higher frequency
I can see the moon and the stars
Smiling back at me
I inhale your new dimension and
You gently kiss my diamond sky
Finally...
I become your Queen and
You become my King

14. After Hours

It's after hours and
We hold hands as we begin to
Beautifully touch lavender skies
Floating in the atmosphere alongside celestial beings
That only you and I can see
Saturating me in pure bliss
You fill me up with your presence
Then we subject ourselves to sensual magical foreplay
You astound me when you look at me
Making my heart skip beats to
Only your majestic gangsta rhythm
You've romanced me for one thousand years
Sending soothing sweet ancient
Endless melodies in my ear
We explore each other's galaxies
While we lie beside the moon unifying our love
Intermingling our King and Queen energies
I sing you a sweet song
That only you can hear and feel
You swim in my turquoise waters so lovely and freely
You make me speak in foreign languages
That only you and I can understand
The intertwining of our souls begin
Finally, we release and
The art of combustion is here
Putting me in a mystical trance
Fascinating me with your overwhelming potency
We are now; forever
Eternally synchronized in love
We become one together
It's after hours, my dear

15. Please Stay

Morning is here and
You are still here with me
The dawn of
A new day
Has sweetly crept in
We lie here together
Lavishing in chocolate
And vanilla bliss
In between wrinkled
Egyptian cotton and silk sheets
Still entangled in love
Drenched in each other's passion
Wrapped up in your arms
I see the sun rays light
Dancing across my windowpane
Sharing my life
With you feels so beautiful
Will you please
Stay with me
One more day
Until the morning sun comes
To greet us again
Please stay with me
For one more day
Please stay

16. Love After 7

Love after 7
Tastes so juicy and sweet
A kaleidoscope of mesmerizing deceit
Is what you give to me
Your enchanting splendor
Keeps my knees trembling and weak
You provide a love so tender
From what I remember
I couldn't deny you if I tried
I crave your decadent flavor
Your strong robust scent
Makes my head spin and yet
You leave my emotions dangling in
Strong alluring catastrophic winds
After three decades
I stand here attempting to
Rewrite our script
Finally, here we go again
Thinking that we should end
Before we tumultuously begin
It's love after 7 once more
My friend

17. Mocha Treat

May I please have one more cup of your soothing mocha latte?
You are my deepest divine cacao blissful pleasure
Spending time with you is a gift that I will always treasure
My warm chill sensual great getaway
My luxurious decadent escape
My delicious deliberate delight
My sweet exotic beautiful sipping dream come true
My infinite tranquility and peace
My chocolate Nubian King
My savored stress reliever and ease
My taste buds are synched in your hot flavorful steam
Creamy smooth hot fudgsicle type rhythmic stream
Your invigorating aroma keeps my soul weak
You simply intoxicate me
A timeless tongue-tantalizing treat
Scrumptiously palate pleasing indeed
My splendid coffee brown Rolls-Royce
My amazing definite desired drink of choice
You offer my mouth a symphony of sensation submerged in reminisce
Mocha treat, you are the one for me

18. Tonight

His eyes stay shining bright on me tonight
Wearing my kinky all-natural hair pinned up
Peep toe heels and a sexy orange linen dress
Contouring and complementing my voluptuous curves from every angle
Succulent honey dew sun-kissed skin
You know that kind right?
The Egyptian Queen blend
Definition in my arms chiseled tight
I got my pretty face on, looking all kinds of fly
Nipples protruding and full breasts sitting up so nice
Wide baby making hips swaying from side to side
Radiating a sultry easy flow type vibe
It's going down tonight
We be on a fantasy love type of high
Candlelight dinner under a seductive fluorescent moon lit night
Men standing by begging for a taste of my sweet delight
Wishing they could get a whiff of my luscious pink strawberry-scented skies
Yep, his eyes stayed shining bright on his diamond
Especially tonight

19. Iridescent Natural Healing Man

I dreamed of you last night
Your beautiful spirit came to me while I was asleep
Your body was translucent with an iridescent majestic glow
Your head was crowned in strength and honor
Adorned with magnificent rubies and gold
You shined brightly from head to toe
You gently washed my natural hair
Then you whispered a soft, beautiful mesmerizing melody in my ear
You meticulously rubbed and massaged my feet
It seemed as if you had an important message for me
I tried to reach out to you but you were already beginning to disappear
Slowly vanishing into the illuminating midnight air
You hold me captive to your alluring mystique
Iridescent healing man, what is it that you seek?
Especially from me

20. I See You

When I looked into your eyes
I saw a shattered empty soul in disguise
I saw fear, dishonesty, resentment, anger, hostility and frustration
Hiding in the cob-webbed corners of your dark mahogany wood-colored eyes
Trying hard not to be seen by me
I saw you anyway
I looked deeply into your eyes trying to see if love lived there or maybe even spent the night and to my surprise
I saw a wolf and a lion all dressed up in sheep's clothing
Little did you know
Your eyes are a representation to the window of your soul
Don't ever think that I can't see you
Pretending to be something that you are not
And yet, you still refuse to see
The man that you need to critique
The truth is fighting you
Struggling and trying to manifest
Wanting to break your chains of bondage and misery
It screams, "I want to set you free"
Gifted eyes can see and recognize real lies
I wasn't looking for perfection
I was only looking for honesty
I guess this is where our friendship ends…
Before it begins…
My love, I still see you

21. Full

I drink from the fountain of love and compassion
My endearing heart pulls me closer towards him
The intoxicating aroma of his chocolate scent
Keeps my soul hungry and begging for more
My senses become aroused and my flesh becomes weak
I am swept into an indulgent blissful fantasy full of illusions
He whispers a soft captivating melody in my ear
Drenched in beautiful notes
I find myself captured by the very essence
Of his enormous web of deceit
I thrive off his heartbeat
Vigorously beating to a wonderful majestic rhythm
I explore every detail of love with him
From every angle and position
We groove to heightened vibrations of ecstasy
Finally, I allow myself to kiss
The universal galaxies of his existence
I no longer crave intimacy
I have satisfied my hunger pangs
I am fulfilled beyond imagination
The sweet taste from his lips activates poetry in motion
Beyond my wildest dreams
I now drink an exotic elixir made from hope
Promises, reminiscences and love

22. The Ultimate

Your masculine silhouette is a display of architectural design
That can never be denied or refined
You are the oxygen that sends
Life and nourishment to my brain
You leave my emotions untamed
You introduce me to high altitudes of intrigue
You mesmerize me with your wondrous gifts
When you look at me, your eyes write Afrocentric scripts
When you kiss me, my tongue recites metaphysics
Your brilliance sends me into another dimension
Beyond the Earth's atmosphere
And now, I find myself engulfed
In your monuments of magnificence

23. You Are Beautiful

I see love in your eyes when you look at me
Your tender kisses seduce me sending me into fields of ecstasy
Your soothing warm breath still cascades along my collarbone
A never-ending tidal wave of love is what I feel whenever I am
near you

Your voice gives me exploding surges of pleasure that flow freely
down my spine
Your sensual aura amuses me and then I become weak…only for you
The memory of your kiss still breathes inside my head like sweet
subtle whispers in the night
Your tender touch gives me flaming flights of fancy making me
crave you more and more
Your sweet masculine scent makes me faint with love
The deep color of your mahogany skin sends me into oblivion
making me forget my name
And yet you continue to leave me dangling out on a string
You are a wonderful dream that never comes true

You are a beautiful memory that fades away with the Sun
I so desperately wish that we could become one
You will forever be my one true love
You are an exquisite masterpiece
Waiting for me in the distance
Like the stars in the sky high above

24. Autumn

It's the first day of Fall
We cuddle and watch
The leaves on our front yard
Tree turn yellowish brown
To bright red orange
Falling on the ground
Returning to the Earth
From whence they came
I can see the sun rising in the East
And setting in the West
We see, feel and smell
Nature running its course
Our ears are wide open
Listening to the voice
Of each other's heartbeat
Everything in our Universe
Starts to align perfectly
Taking the road less traveled
We follow our dreams respectively
Accepting each other's differences
And passionately falling in
Love with our similarities
No longer drifting through
The heavens trying
To find our identity
You become a reflection of me
You dance to the beat
Of my every wish and
Then you make them
All come true
And I do the same
For you

Together we reach
A lover's equinox
Following the compass
Of our beautiful hearts
Finally
Autumn is here

25. A Love Supreme

You make each moment feel sacred
Touching me in places I didn't know exist
Giving me unfathomable experiences
More than my mind could ever comprehend
Playing with my intelligence
When you make love to me
You go beyond what could ever
Possibly be understood or imagined
Making sweet pineapple-infused lemonade
Tears pour from my light brown colored eyes
I watch and feel you taste each teardrop with
Your beautiful exploring soft and delicate tongue
I love the way you touch every inch of my flesh
You gently plunge in and out and
Off to wonderland we go
You grab a hold of my hand
Then you set me free so wonderfully
You simply take my breath away
Leaving me vulnerable at the whim
Of your every beckoning call
The way you love me mirrors my religion
Our love transcends into profound art
Leaving behind a legacy of phenomena
And blueprints for our children to emulate
You have always been my physical equal
Sweetly scattering my morning dew
Keeping my body aligned to only you
You were made for me to love
And I am designed just for you
Stuck to each other indefinitely
Immersed in lovers glue
True love withstanding the test of time

You make me love you in a place
Where there is no heaven or earth
It's only you and I
Eternally

26. The Way You Love Me

I love the way you Queen me
I love the way you honor and respect me
I love the way you protect me
I love the way you work hard for me

I love the way you embrace me
I love the way you gift and shower me
I love the way you entice me
I love the way you stare at me

I love the way you appreciate me
I love the way you cook dinner for me
I love the way you still court me
I love the way you dance for me

I love the way you undress me
I love the way you tickle me
I love the way you comfort me
I love the way you help to complete me

I love the way you intrigue me
I love the way you shine with me
I love the way your smile captivates me
I love the way you seduce me
I love the way you pleasure me
More importantly, I love the way
You know how to love me

27. You Left a Stain On Me

You left a stain on me
You did it so very carelessly
Haunted by visions of you while my days slowly slip into twilight
Wondering if this pain will ever take flight
Unfulfilled dreams but aspirations still in sight
All polished up during daylight
Still, I cry myself to sleep at night
My soul anxiously awaits thee
After all this time, why do I miss you so much
Looking in the mirror trying to figure out where we went wrong
Constantly listening to these sad-ass love songs
My body is still longing for your touch
Remembering how you used to make my cheeks get all flushed
We unconsciously ran out of time
Something we can never get back or find
No matter what I do, I can't seem to forget about you
I wonder if you feel the same way about me too
Damn, I keep trying to wipe this stain clean
It won't come out
Turning my white chiffon dress into a dirty shade of gray
Afraid to step outside for fear of what others might say
Wondering if they can tell that
I am still in love with you
Damn, I keep trying wipe this stain clean but
It won't come out
You left a permanent stain on me that only my eyes can see

28. A Hole in My Soul

I gave you my heart to keep forever
You gave me your backside to kiss
I made you my priority and
One of my most prized possessions
In return
You gave me neglect,
Dishonor and disrespect
I told you that I loved you
I wanted to be with you forever
But you shrugged your shoulders
& then you smiled and had the audacity
To laugh in my face
I told you that you really hurt me
You said, "I don't believe you"
I said okay and showed you
All of the marks and bruises
You left on my arm and neck
The night before
I told you I was a woman of great worth
But you continued to ignore me
I told you that
You left a hole in my soul
You said, "Oh well"
So, I said farewell
Forever
You left a black
Deep hole in my soul

29. Homage

You hold me close to your chest…
My nostrils hungrily embrace the freshness of
Your overpowering chocolate-covered strawberry scent
The mere thought of your sweetness
Sends my mouth into salivation overload
My body instantaneously responds
Without my permission
With each kiss you anoint me
Into my higher calling
Giving me instant waves of insurmountable
Gratification and bliss
Constantly wooing me
With your charismatic persistence
And your sultry fierce
One of a kind intellect
Appeasing my savage hunger
With your strong masculinity
Making me soar into my passions
I now go beyond what
I could not have ever envisioned
Myself doing or becoming and
Because of your return
I am now living my true life
Calling and my dreams
I repay you with homage
You become my
Libation for poetry
I have loved you since the
Beginning of time
You have always belonged to me
And I have always loved only you
You give me loyalty and
I give you a lifetime

30. Adornment and Envy

You shower me with
Black diamonds, red rubies and
Lovely chocolate pearls
Sitting me next to you
On your purple royal throne
You give me the moon
And stars as birthday gifts
Then you place a beautiful crown of emeralds, blue
Sapphires and turquois jewels upon my head
You adorn my wrist with bronze and then
You turn my clear waters into radiant
Pure liquid gold
You cater to my
Every need and want
You make all the haters fume with envy
I see the looks and
Stares they give me
Lost and miserable
Scalawag souls driving recklessly and
Hysterically attempting to run me off the road
Drooling, howling and lurking
In the background
Trying to plot my demise
I think to myself…damn
They must be miserable at home
The foolishness humors me
Stay in your lane
One false move my
Nina is prepared and
Ready to smoke
I will protect my
Foundation relentlessly so

Don't let this light
Skin color fool you
They can't seem to
Understand that you
Are a one-woman man
I guess they hate to
See the beautiful swans in our pool
That you so freely provide for me
Sharing my life with
You feels so sweet
Like a delicious never-ending
Palate pleasing passion fruit treat
You provide a lifestyle
That most women would do
Backward flips to be in
You carry me into the
Threshold of love infinitely
Never in my life did
I think I would find
Someone as splendid
You are my king and
My dream maker
I am your queen
Who will continue to
Lay your golden eggs

31. Awakening

You awaken me with
A soft gentle forehead kiss
Bestowing a beautiful halo
Teasing my consciousness
Making me recognize the
Purpose for our journey
You help me fill an infinite void
You give oxygen to the
Thoughts that live inside my brain
And now they take flight
Flowing with depth
Changing my atmosphere
Sending my DNA to a
Higher realm of intelligence
My spiritual awareness starts to ascend
I can feel my life span increasing
I can see the colors turquoise,
yellow and orange radiating from my skin
My flesh starts to glow and glisten
Making me shine brightly
You've got me feeling carefree
Like a sweet raspberry-flavored
Kiss floating in the wind
Now the whole world can see
I am no longer asleep
I become epically me
Understanding my being
I now realize my purpose
You assist the universe with
Orchestrating my life's path
I am love coming forth from within
Thank you for helping

Me beautifully begin
I will always remember and
Keep a candle lit for
You, my dear friend

32. Engage Me

Your beautiful image transcends throughout time and space
Your ripped definition is a gesture of pure pleasure
Your intriguing skin color captivates me
Your body is simply flawless and
Very pleasing to the natural naked eye
A fortress of mesmerizing eye candy
You fascinate me with your expeditious physique
A magnitude of wonderful endless possibilities
The structure of your anatomy engulfs me
You are an amazing magnificent machine
A brilliant spectacular instrument
A finely tuned sculpted
Leonardo da Vinci Masterpiece
Your earth suit is astonishing
You savagely invade my imaginations with
Intoxicating thoughts of you
You lead me to illusions of mind-blowing ecstasy
Then you become my ritual
And the ceremony begins
You satisfy me in beautiful explosive volcanic clouds of dreams
Making me gush streams of fiery hot lava
Full throttle overflow
I am extremely attracted to your splendor
Let me be a part of your legacy
Will you please
Engage me

33. My Thoughts

Element of majestic masculine beauty
Forcefully penetrating and invading my mind with
Intense stimulating thoughts of you
The scent of your cologne still
Lingers in the air I breathe
Floating in the atmosphere

I so love that seducing musk fragrance you wear
Always teasing me without even trying
Your tongue play is simply divine
Kissing me in all the right spots
Sending my body into total incline

How can I ever deny myself
When it comes to you?
Complicating the simplicity of my life
Making me second guess myself
Blowing in your strong gusts of alluring winds
Constantly seeping in through
The crevices of my broken windowpane

My flesh desperately craves you
A mystical light surrounds your body
It radiates off your face
Glistening through and through
There is no escape
I am addicted to you

34. Beautiful Alchemy

When I close my eyes
I can still see
Your beautiful face
I sleep awake waiting
For you to call me I
Anticipate the sound
Of the phone ringing
Your strong inner "G"
Makes me succumb
To the deep tone
Of your voice I hang
On to every word you speak
You always seem to know
Exactly what I'm thinking
I can see and feel you
Multidimensionally
You liberate my soul
And energize my dreams
The scent of your skin
Permeates my nostrils
Like the sweet smell
Of candy apple perfume
There is never a dull
Moment when I am
In your presence you
Make statements without
Knowing or trying you
Connect me to my core
Which allows me to
Freely express my
Lovely elevated finer
Cultivated self with

Gratitude grace and ease
You make me see all
The beautiful colors
Of love with my eyes
Closed wide open shut

35. Blind Love

They say love is blind
But you are the only
Person on this earth
That I can love with
My eyelids closed
You make it so
Difficult for me to
Love you and every time
I try to stop your
Beautiful heart keeps
Beckoning me, it's stubborn
It won't leave me be
Everyone keeps telling me that
The love I have for you is
Nothing more than an illusion
They all seem to think its blind love
And if it is, so be it
I will forever love only you even if
I must continue to love you with my eyes closed
Wide open shut

36. Chocolate Fairy Tale Man

You make me feel weightless
Just like a soft rose petal
Floating on top of water
The love you give me
Resonates deep within
My consciousness
Giving light to a
Place where uncertainty
And darkness once lived
You make all of my
Fairy tales come to life
Bringing everything I've ever
Dreamed of to fruition
We beautifully align
In every possible way
Flowing in perfect
Synchronistic bliss
I adore how you
Sweep me off my feet
I savor every moment
When I am with you
I fall head over heels
You simply carry me away
Into another time and space
And you forever will
I love you deeply
Chocolate
Fairy tale man

37. Colors

I see so many beautiful colors
In your handsome face
Especially when I look at you
Through blue-tinted shades
You have such a beautiful hue
You make my love dictionary explode
In every possible way
You astound me
Your sweet kisses simply blow me away
Forever and a day

38. Damn, I Must Be Trippin

You are a beautiful specimen
Heaven sent, I must admit
You don't have to say a word
I already know what you're thinking
We be like telekinesis
Damn, I must be trippin'
You exemplify splendor
A love so tender
I remember way back when
I used to feel your heartbeat
I am still digging your toned physique
Come fly with me
Damn, I must be trippin'
Together we can reign supreme
Ecstasy guaranteed
Only for you and me
Your sweet personality continues
To knock me off my feet
Your sexy composition completes
My definition of you
Come soar with me into
The depths of unfamiliarity
I am a queen and you are a king
So hold on to me tight
This is not a dream
This is reality
You keep me on a natural high
Let's touch the sky
Floating into the abyss of love infinitely
You left your blueprints inscribed
Between my thighs
I am ready for you to make

A claim to this and
I need you to put
Your last name on it
Now look into my eyes
And tell me what you see
Damn, I must be trippin'

39. Give Me You

You are my forbidden fruit
Let me taste of you
I desperately anticipate your
Delicious succulent flavor
You initiate love so sweetly
You mesmerize and
Hypnotize me with
The slightest touch
You are intoxicating and
Gratifying at the same time
I long to hold you in my arms
Just to kiss you again
I crave your strong masculine scent
My love, please give me
All of you once more

40. Hardworking Brotha

You are a king in my eyes
I love the way you walk
I love the way you talk to me
I love your strong masculine scent

Hardworking Brotha

I love your humor and your wit
I love your chocolate glow
I love your style and the way you profile
Especially when you want to impress me
You impress me without even trying

Hardworking Brotha

I love your strong physique
I love the strength in your voice
I love the hair on your face
I love your mustache and your goatee

I love your intelligence
I love your brilliance
I love the way you make
Love to my heart
I love the way you say my name

Hardworking Brotha

I love the way you rock your haircut
I love the way you brush your teeth
I love the way you wash your face
I love the way you taste me
With your steep slanted eyes

Hardworking Brotha

I love your tenderness
I love your chill disposition
I love your sexy smile
I love your unapologetic swag

Hardworking Brotha...
I love you

41. I See You, King

I can see all the beauty
That lies within you
I love your strength
And the tight definition
Of your beautifully
Sculpted mahogany-
Colored arms
The texture of
Your skin fascinates
Every delicate fiber
Of my goddess being
You are every womb/mans
Living fantasy and dream
I see your brilliance
I see your courage
I see your drive
I see your ambition
I see your focus
I see your dedication
I see your work ethic
I see your full lips
I see and feel your loyalty
I see your flared nose
Big hands and big feet
I see the strength of our
Ancestors in your melanin skin and
Muscular broad shoulders
It's easy to see
Why they are afraid
And fueled by hate
Everyone knows that
You reign supreme

In everything that you do
You are a magnificent
Hue/Man Being
I see the God in you
I see greatness in you
I see you, king

42. Kiss Me Slowly

Nibble on my ear until
You make me giggle
Kiss me slowly
Sniff me all over until
You make the tiny hairs at the
Nape of my neck stand
Up to attention
Kiss me slowly
Hug me tight as if
You never want me
To leave your sight
Put your fingers on the
Small of my back
Kiss me slowly
Play in my long kinky
Hair until I fall asleep
When I awake, I
Want you to gently
Kiss me slowly
Let's pour chocolate body
Paint all over each other
And give each other a
Soothing back massage
With a nice foot rub
Kiss me slowly
Hold my hand when
We make love look
Into my brown eyes and
When the morning comes
Kiss me slowly
Push me up against
The living room wall

Grab my cheeks with
Both hands then I want you to
Kiss me slowly
Sit quietly with me
For one hour and read
Your favorite book
When you are done
We can exchange pleasantries
Kiss me slowly
At sunrise let's pray together
Meditate and eat
Breakfast outside on
Our top porch balcony
We can have mimosas
Spinach cheese
Eggs with homemade
Lemon curd Pancakes
Turkey bacon with my delicious
Homemade blueberry jam
Afterwards, later in the evening
Just before the clouds
Hide the moon I want you to
Explore the roof of my mouth
With your sweet delicate tongue and
Kiss Me Slowly

43. Kissed

He kissed me as
If he was stuck
In a messy pool
Of old dirty water
He kissed me as if
I was the rescue
Breath of fresh air
That he had been
Desperately longing to
Breathe
He kissed me as if
He knew beyond a
Shadow of a doubt
I was giving him life
He kissed me as if
He knew that I
Could stimulate his
Beautiful intuitive mind
He kissed me as if he
Had traveled back into
Time and retrieved his
Wife
He kissed me as if
I was the universe
Who came for his
Rebirth
He kissed me as if
He finally received his
Lovely shining pot of
Gold
He kissed me as if
He finally realized that

He was a true King who
Knew he had found his
Queen
He kissed me like he
Knew that I was a
Rare gift to be betrothed

44. Mystique

I know you see me
'Cause I see you too
Naturally fly is who I be
A goddess of intrigue
I'm not like the rest I am
Authenticity at its best
Never a copycat
I create my own format
Talented multifaceted in
Every possible way and
Powerful like the sun ray
I was born for greatness
To all those who hate
You can keep that shade
I see it all in your face
Them frown lines on your
Forehead left a trace
My queendom is Zion I
Travel with big black lions
I even conquer giants I am
One of a kind and absolutely
Guaranteed to blow your mind
My luminous melanin skin
Is beautiful and divine
I come from a different creed
Not like any other you've seen
I dwell with queens that
Are extremely unique
Kings bow when I speak
Nations topple at my feet
I am magical and mystical
My kinky Afrocentric hair

Can defy all gravity
I'm staying right here in your face
For you and your people to see
So don't let me catch you asleep
You might as well get
Comfortable and take a seat
I got more coming
For your eyes to feast
I know you feel me
My Name Is Mystique

45. Collaboration

Our energies merge together as one
We become harmoniously united
The dance of intertwine begins
We embrace each other
Synergies start to connect from every angle
Liberating and caressing our creative souls
Aligning earth, wind, water and fire
Sitting on top of stars
We watch the moon make
Beautiful passionate love to the sun
Then we prepare for the ride of our lives
You take me on the most
Amazing solar system flight
Then we humbly kiss monuments of the
Universal galaxies
We learn how to fly

46. Spare Key

Just when you thought
You had him on lock
Just when you thought
You had shattered his
Self-esteem and that
He could no longer
Dream of becoming
His greatest higher being
Just when you thought
He would never leave
Just when you thought
He was uncertain and
Afraid to venture out
Little did you know
He had always known
Deep in his heart that
There was something
So very precious and
So very beautiful
Waiting in the evening
Wind to cheer him
On with an old
Refined familiar
Golden spare key

47. Summertime Loveliness

Beauty in full bloom
Natural kinky breeze blown hair
Endless love
Intelligent conversations
Ripe summer berries
Homemade spices & jams
Peach cobbler pound cake
Serenading poetry
Rising sunsets
Sunny afternoon clouds
Spiritual connectedness
Handmade soaps &
Whipped shea butters
Sniffs on the collarbone
Green haze smoke
Feel good pain
Old school classics
Long walks by the shore
Knowing the unknown
Sun-kissed skin
Rustic hotel rooms
Peruvian late night dinners
Bed & breakfast inns
Sweet fruity wine
Euphoric kisses
The plumpness of
Full breasts in a
White linen and
Lace tube top
Sultry sundresses
Rain showers In July
Caramel-colored eyes

A delicate touch at the tip of the tailbone
Warm whispers in the ear
Beautiful landscapes
Birds chirping in the air
Natural full-bearded men
White glistening teeth
Early morning
Windowpane dew
Foreign friends with
Distant listening ears
Evening horse carriage rides
Girlfriend's bliss
Nature's nectar
Grilled watermelon skewers
Ice-cold tart lemonade
Tongue flickering licks
Honesty at its best
Rooftop lunch dates
Caribbean boat trips

48. Sweet Delivery

I love the way you
Sweetly surprise me
Always catching me
Off guard with
Unannounced spur-of-
The-moment afternoon
Rendezvous and fancy
Fun-filled picnics I
Love the pretty lavender
Dinnerware and the bubbly
Pink champagne the
Presentation is immaculate
And beautiful
You have a very refined
And acquired taste
It's amazing how you
Always know exactly
What to do by making
The best of everything
Especially the moments
We share together
Wooing and intoxicating
Me with your sensual
Purposeful priming
And use of sleek
Language tones
To disarm me
When you kiss me I
Can see cirrus clouds
And watercolors
In your eyes
I can also see a

A fascinating colorful
Aurora Borealis
Staring back at me
You ensure decadence with
Every delicious kiss
Giving my mouth an intense
Concentration of sweet
Tangy and freshness
Your tongue is juicy
Velvety smooth and fruity
With subtle green candy
Apple overtones an
Exceptional opulent palate
Pleasing delightful gift
You leave my mouth
Bursting with sensation
And flavor making my
Salivary glands beg
And plead for more
I am wildly uncontrollably
Attracted to your splendor
You make my lips
And teeth quiver
You are a well-seasoned
Distinct craftsman
You impress me with flair
And chivalry which allows
Me to feel you with
My heart and my soul
You make me resolve
To do more of the things
That make me happy
My beauty is a
Reflection of you
Ordinary days are always

Beautiful and magical
When I am with you
I can always find
My place of contentment
I think of you with
Each breath I take
I get carried away
With the very
Essence of you
You make my thoughts
Travel to the ends of
The earth and
This is why I will
Always love you
I love your sweet
Delivery

49. Warrior Queen

They see illuminating
Beauty all over my body
They fear me because they
Can see the divine source
God energy uplifting me
Multiplying my senses
Brilliantly transforming me
Restoring my youth
Building my muscle
Enabling me to stand strong
And firm in the
Presence of any adversary
Torturing them with
Fascinating mind-blowing
Intelligence bestowed upon
Me as a birthright
An ancient ancestral inheritance
A gift that I continue to
Wholeheartedly receive
I move mountains with
Heavy words
Disrobing them with sophisticated
Nouns and verbs
Power driving them
Into the ground with
My sultry sexiness
Got them swirling and
Twirling in tropical
Cyclones trying to
Figure me out
They be looking at me
With mouths all twisted

Their entire face in a pout
Envying what they don't understand
Setting their ears on
Fire and making their
Eyes jump out of sockets
No need to lay hands
I will continue to conquer
With my genius and my
Inner Super WO/MAN
I am a warrior queen
A camouflaged sharpshooter
Still in training

50. Sitting Pretty

I will patiently wait for you
And sit pretty just like
The beautiful moon
That sits quietly
Over the city of Monaco

51. Sweet Just Like 16

Yep, that was me
With that pretty
Sweet oval face
Back in the day when
I lived in the hood on
A street called Center
& 24th Place
I was sixteen, sweet young
Pure and tender
Beautiful sun-kissed skin
That was delicate
Fluffy and soft
I can still remember
Visiting my best friend
Dancing in her backyard
Treehouse loft
My cheeks were always
Red especially during
The cold chilly winter months
So precious and free
Running free with the
Wind in my hair
Dancing in the rain
With high yellow cheekbones
& Narrow bare feet
Bright-eyed just
Like the sun
Couldn't wait to
Get outside just
So I could have fun
Summertime was always
A special treat

I can still hear
Momma calling me
Yelling "Brenda come home
Before the street
Lights come on"
Momma made sure I
Stayed in the house
Until my homework
Was completely done
I would often find myself
Going to the corner
Store to purchase
Strawberry- and lemon-
Flavored lip balm
Sneaking and hiding in
The back hallway
With my high school
Crush getting my first
Mind-blowing kiss
A naive fragile queen
Smelling like bubble gum
Cherry licorice mixed
With vanilla ice cream
A star child indeed
My mother's dream
Yep, that's me
Back in the day
On Center Street
Sweet just like 16

52. Girl, Stop Tripping

Girl, don't be silly
I don't want your man
I'm just having a lil
Fun with him because I can
It's no secret that
He likes to flirt
We both know
I had him first
I could take him
Away from you if
I really wanted to
He will always
Be my boo
I thought you knew
I would like
To teach you
One thing or two
On what you
Need to do
Cause he keeps
Trying to stick
To me like glue
Girl, don't worry
I will give him
Back to you
When I'm through
It's no big thing
It's just a fling
Girl, stop tripping

53. Honor

I take great pleasure
In honoring and
Serving only you
You are my king
I am your queen
I am your backbone
You are my strength
I will continue to
Hold you up
So that you and I
Can continue to fly

54. Please Forgive Me

When I first saw you
I just had to have you
We were lovers before we became friends
I only wanted you, there were no others
Please forgive me
I gave you husband benefits without
Requiring you to put in the work
Damn, I was so young and naïve
Remembering this chapter of my life still hurts
I often think about you and what our life
Would have been like if we were still together
I imagined us having two or three children
A big beautiful house
And a shiny black Mercedes-Benz
We made each other promises
That abruptly came to a sad end
A tragic end
Please Forgive Me
I was with child
I felt abandoned, alone and afraid
When I needed you the most
You didn't make a sound
Instead you left me all by myself
In a dark, lonely and destitute land
Called only for the dumbfound
I guess you were probably
Trying to find yourself
It's not that I was selfish
I just loved you
More than breathing air
And life itself
Shame on me for not knowing any better

As a result, a terrible decision was made
It is forever carved in my heart
God only knows to this very day
I am still paying for that horrible mistake
Please Forgive Me
You were my everything
And unfortunately, you didn't even know it
I desperately wanted to be your first priority
But instead you chose to make me
One of your options
I tried so very hard to see through
All of your imperfections
But, when I looked in the mirror
I only saw my reflection
You promised me that nothing
Would ever tear us apart
Our love began with a single kiss
And it ended with ten million blood stained teardrops
Can you please forgive me...

This poem is dedicated to Baby Aquarius Williams

This poem is also dedicated to my Mother Ms. Ella Mae Williams
who helped me during a difficult period of my life. RIP Momma,
my love for you goes beyond the grave and beyond the earth's
atmosphere. I love you eternally Ms. Ella Mae Williams.

CPSIA information can be obtained
at www.ICGtesting.com
Printed in the USA
BVHW071317260521
608177BV00002B/355